PLEASURE GREEN

GUMROAD MONEY MAKING: Unlocking Earnings for Digital Entrepreneurs and Gateway to Online Sales

Table of Contents

INTRODUCTION

Gumroad is an online platform that has gained popularity as a digital marketplace and e-commerce solution for creators and artists. Founded in 2011 by Sahil Lavingia, Gumroad provides a user-friendly, versatile, and easy-to-use platform for individuals and businesses to sell a wide range of digital products directly to their audience.

Creators across various domains, including writers, artists, musicians, designers, software developers, and more, use Gumroad to monetize their digital creations, whether it be e-books, music, artwork, software, online courses, or any other digital content. Gumroad's versatility makes it a valuable tool for anyone looking to distribute their work and connect with their fans or customers.

One of Gumroad's defining features is its flexibility and simplicity. It allows creators to set their own prices, choose different payment methods, and offer various types of products, including one-time purchases, subscriptions, or pre-orders. Gumroad's user-friendly interface makes it easy to upload and showcase digital content, and it also offers tools for marketing and audience engagement.

Gumroad is known for its transparent pricing structure, where creators pay a small fee and a percentage of sales for using the platform. This straightforward approach enables creators to keep more of their earnings while leveraging Gumroad's features and support to grow their businesses.

In addition to being a marketplace, Gumroad also offers features like email integration, analytics, and customizable sales pages to help creators reach a wider audience and track their progress.

Whether you're a seasoned professional or just starting your journey as a creator, Gumroad is a platform that empowers individuals and small businesses to share and sell their digital products while building a direct connection with their audience. It continues to play a significant role in the digital creator economy, providing a bridge between creators and their supporters in a straightforward and accessible way.

CREATING AND SELLING DIGITAL PRODUCTS

Creating and selling digital products is a fundamental aspect of utilizing platforms like Gumroad to monetize your skills and creativity. Here's a more detailed exploration of this subtopic:

Choosing Your Digital Product

- Select a niche or category for your digital product, such as e-books, artwork, music, software, online courses, templates, or any other type of digital content.
- Research market demand and competition to identify opportunities in your chosen niche.

Content Creation and Development

- Plan and outline your digital product, considering its structure, format, and content.
- Use appropriate tools and software to create your digital content, whether it's writing software, graphic design tools, music production software, or others.

Quality and Presentation

- Ensure your digital product is of high quality, with professional design and presentation.
- Use visuals, cover art, or branding that make your product visually appealing and stand out.

Pricing and Packaging

- Determine the pricing strategy for your digital product, considering factors like production costs, market value, and the perceived value to customers.
- Decide on packaging options, such as offering different versions, bundles, or bonus content to entice buyers.

File Formats and Delivery

- Choose the appropriate file formats for your digital product, considering compatibility and ease of use for customers.
- Set up a reliable delivery system, whether it's through Gumroad's built-in delivery options, third-party tools, or custom solutions.

Protecting Your Digital Products

- Implement security measures to protect your digital products from piracy and unauthorized distribution.
- Consider using DRM or watermarking for added security.

Metadata and Descriptions

- Create compelling and informative product descriptions, including keywords that make your product discoverable.
- Use relevant metadata and tags to help potential customers find your product through search and category listings.

Preview and Samples

- Offer previews, sample chapters, or excerpts to give potential buyers a taste of your digital product.
- Use this as an opportunity to engage and hook your audience.

Iterative Improvement

- Continuously assess and improve your digital product based on customer feedback and evolving market trends.
- Consider launching updates or new editions to keep your product fresh.

Legal Considerations

- Ensure that your digital product doesn't infringe on copyright or intellectual property rights.
- Create and use licenses if necessary to specify usage rights for customers.

Creating a Sales Page on Gumroad

- Utilize Gumroad's features to create an attractive sales page for your product, complete with descriptions, visuals, and pricing options.
- Use customizations to match your branding and style.

Market Research and Audience Targeting

- Identify your target audience and create marketing strategies tailored to their needs and interests.
- Analyze market trends and adapt your product offerings accordingly.

Feedback and Reviews

- Encourage customers to leave reviews and provide feedback on your product.

- Use positive reviews as testimonials and constructive feedback for product improvement.

Launch and Promotion

- Plan a product launch strategy, including pre-launch promotion to build anticipation.
- Use social media, email marketing, and other channels to promote your digital product.

Customer Support and Communication

- Provide excellent customer support to address inquiries and resolve issues promptly.
- Use Gumroad's communication features to keep customers informed about updates, new products, and special offers.

Creating and selling digital products on Gumroad can be a rewarding endeavor for creators, entrepreneurs, and artists. It involves a mix of creative content development, technical considerations, marketing, and ongoing engagement with your audience. By mastering these aspects, you can successfully monetize your digital creations on the platform.

MARKETING AND PROMOTION

Marketing and promotion are crucial aspects of successfully selling your digital products on Gumroad. Here are some key strategies and considerations to effectively market and promote your products:

Understanding Your Target Audience

- Define your ideal customer or audience. Understand their needs, preferences, and pain points.
- Create buyer personas to better tailor your marketing efforts.

Content Marketing

- Create valuable, informative, or entertaining content related to your niche. This can include blog posts, videos, podcasts, or social media content.
- Share your content on various platforms to establish yourself as an authority in your field and attract a following.

Email Marketing

- Build and maintain an email list of potential customers and existing buyers.
- Send regular newsletters with updates, special offers, and engaging content to keep your audience informed and engaged.

Social Media Marketing

- Leverage social media platforms like Facebook, Twitter, Instagram, and LinkedIn to promote your products.
- Create engaging posts, use relevant hashtags, and interact with your audience.

Search Engine Optimization (SEO)

- Optimize your Gumroad product listings and website for search engines to improve discoverability.
- Use relevant keywords, meta descriptions, and alt text for images.

Paid Advertising

- Consider running paid advertising campaigns on platforms like Google Ads, Facebook Ads, or Instagram Ads to reach a broader audience.
- Set a budget and target your ads to specific demographics or interests.

Influencer Marketing

- Collaborate with influencers or content creators in your niche to promote your products.
- Influencers can help you tap into their established audiences and provide authentic recommendations.

Content Distribution

- Share your digital products on content-sharing platforms like Medium, YouTube, or SlideShare.
- Cross-promote your Gumroad store and products through these platforms.

Partnerships and Cross-Promotion

- Partner with other creators or businesses in related niches for cross-promotion.

- Run joint promotions or campaigns to reach each other's audiences.

Leverage Customer Reviews and Testimonials

- Use positive customer reviews and testimonials to build trust and social proof.
- Feature these reviews prominently on your Gumroad product pages.

Limited-Time Offers and Discounts

- Create a sense of urgency by offering limited-time discounts or promotions.
- Communicate the value of your product and the savings customers will receive.

Webinars and Online Events

- Host webinars, online workshops, or virtual events related to your products.
- Use these events to educate your audience and showcase your expertise.

Affiliate Marketing

- Set up an affiliate program to encourage others to promote your products in exchange for a commission.
- Use Gumroad's affiliate tools to track and manage these partnerships.

Analytics and A/B Testing

- Use analytics tools to track the performance of your marketing efforts.
- Conduct A/B testing to refine your strategies and optimize your marketing campaigns.

Consistent Branding

- Maintain a consistent and recognizable brand image across all your marketing materials.
- This includes your Gumroad store, website, social media profiles, and email campaigns.

Customer Engagement and Community Building

- Foster a sense of community around your products by engaging with customers on social media, in forums, or through online communities.

- Encourage user-generated content and customer discussions.

Customer Loyalty Programs

- Reward loyal customers with exclusive offers, early access, or special bonuses.
- Encourage repeat business and referrals.

Measuring ROI and Adjusting Strategies

- Monitor the return on investment (ROI) for your marketing efforts.
- Be prepared to adjust your strategies based on what is working and what isn't.

Feedback and Iteration

- Listen to customer feedback and make improvements based on their suggestions.
- Show your commitment to enhancing the customer experience.

Effective marketing and promotion are ongoing processes. It's essential to track your results, adapt to changing market conditions, and continuously refine your strategies to maximize your sales on Gumroad.

MANAGING YOUR GUMROAD STORE

Managing your Gumroad store is crucial for successfully selling digital products and providing a positive customer experience. Here's a detailed breakdown of how to effectively manage your Gumroad store:

Setting Up Your Store

- Create a Gumroad account and set up your store profile, including your store name, logo, and branding.
- Customize your store page to match your brand's identity and style.

Product Listings

- Add your digital products to your Gumroad store, including titles, descriptions, pricing, and product details.
- Upload product files, whether they are e-books, music tracks, software, or other digital content.
- Specify product categories and use relevant tags to improve discoverability.

Pricing and Payment Options

- Define the pricing strategy for your products, including setting fixed prices, pay-what-you-want pricing, or free downloads.

- Configure payment options and methods, such as credit card payments, PayPal, and Apple Pay.

Managing Inventory

- Keep track of your digital product inventory to ensure you have sufficient files available for immediate delivery.

- Consider adding limited-time or exclusive releases to create urgency.

Analytics and Reporting

- Use Gumroad's built-in analytics to monitor sales, customer demographics, and product performance.

- Analyze customer behavior and sales trends to make informed decisions.

Sales Pages

- Create visually appealing and informative sales pages for each product in your store.

- Use multimedia elements, such as images, videos, and interactive content, to engage potential customers.

Product Updates

- Regularly update your digital products to fix issues, provide new content, or address customer feedback.
- Inform customers about updates and improvements.

Email Marketing Integration

- Connect your Gumroad store with email marketing platforms to automate email campaigns and newsletters.
- Use this integration to keep your audience informed about new products and updates.

Customer Support and Inquiries

- Monitor and respond to customer inquiries, comments, and feedback in a timely and professional manner.
- Provide excellent customer support to address any issues or questions.

Refunds and Returns

- Establish a clear refund and return policy for your digital products.

- Process refunds or returns promptly and with a customer-centric approach.

Tax and Legal Compliance

- Ensure your Gumroad store complies with tax laws and regulations relevant to your location and the locations of your customers.

- Keep accurate records for tax reporting purposes.

Growth and Scaling

- Continuously explore opportunities for scaling your store, such as adding new products, expanding into related niches, or offering bundled products.

- Consider automating aspects of your store management as it grows.

Customer Engagement

- Engage with your audience on social media and through email marketing.

- Use updates, newsletters, and exclusive offers to keep customers engaged and informed.

Marketing and Promotions

- Plan and execute marketing campaigns to drive traffic to your Gumroad store.
- Promote your products on various platforms and through different marketing channels.

Third-Party Integrations

- Explore third-party integrations and tools that can enhance your Gumroad store's functionality.
- Integrate tools for analytics, customer support, email marketing, and more.

User Experience Optimization

- Regularly evaluate the user experience on your Gumroad store, ensuring it's user-friendly, mobile-responsive, and easy to navigate.
- Make improvements based on user feedback and analytics.

Data Security and Privacy

- Protect customer data and maintain strict data security and privacy measures.
- Stay compliant with data protection regulations, such as GDPR and CCPA.

Collaborations and Partnerships

- Explore collaboration opportunities with other creators, businesses, or affiliates to cross-promote products and extend your reach.

Effective management of your Gumroad store involves ongoing attention to details, customer satisfaction, and adaptation to market changes. By continuously refining your store's operations and customer interactions, you can optimize your sales and build a loyal customer base.

PAYMENT PROCESSING AND FEES

Understanding payment processing and fees on Gumroad is crucial for creators and sellers using the platform. Gumroad offers a straightforward fee structure for processing payments and selling digital products. Here's an in-depth look at payment processing and fees on Gumroad:

Transaction Fees

Gumroad charges a transaction fee on each sale. As of my last knowledge update in 2022, this fee typically consists of a 5% fee per transaction, plus an additional fee of $0.25 per transaction. Keep in mind that these fees may vary, so it's essential to check Gumroad's official website for the most current rates.

Payouts and Payment Schedule

Sellers receive payouts from Gumroad through their chosen payout method. Gumroad supports direct bank deposits (ACH in the US and international wire transfers) and PayPal.

Payouts are typically processed every Friday, but there is a seven-day hold on payments for new accounts. This means that for the first week, your earnings will be held before they are included in your payout.

Currency Conversion and Additional Fees

If you are selling to customers in different currencies, Gumroad will convert the sale amount to your selected payout currency at the prevailing exchange rate. Currency conversion fees may apply, depending on your payout method and the financial institutions involved.

Chargebacks and Refunds

If a customer requests a chargeback or refund, Gumroad will deduct the refund amount, including any associated fees, from your Gumroad balance. Sellers are responsible for managing customer disputes and refunds.

Payment Gateway Fees

In addition to Gumroad's transaction fees, payment gateway fees may apply. These are fees charged by the financial institutions or payment processors that handle credit card transactions. The specific fees depend on the payment method used by the customer.

Tax Withholding and Reporting

Gumroad does not withhold taxes for you, so sellers are responsible for reporting their earnings and paying taxes in accordance with their local tax regulations. Keep accurate records of your earnings for tax reporting purposes.

Access to Earnings

Earnings from sales on Gumroad are typically available for withdrawal seven days after a successful sale. However, this timeframe may be subject to change, so it's essential to review the most up-to-date information on the Gumroad website.

Handling Fees for Pre-orders and Subscriptions

Pre-orders and subscription-based products on Gumroad may have different fee structures or handling processes. Be sure to understand the specific details when setting up such products.

Gumroad Pro and Custom Plans

Gumroad offers a Pro subscription plan and custom plans with additional features for creators. Depending on the plan, you may have access to lower transaction fees and more advanced analytics. Review Gumroad's pricing page for details on these plans.

Please note that the information provided here is based on my knowledge as of 2022, and Gumroad's fee structure or policies may have evolved since then. Therefore, it's important to visit Gumroad's official website or contact their support for the most current information on payment processing and fees before setting up your Gumroad store. Understanding these fees and the payment process is essential for accurately pricing your products and managing your finances on the platform.

LEGAL AND COPYRIGHT CONSIDERATIONS

Legal and copyright considerations are essential when creating and selling digital products on platforms like Gumroad. Here's an in-depth exploration of the key legal and copyright aspects you should be aware of:

Copyright and Intellectual Property Rights

- Ensure that you have the legal right to sell the digital products you offer on Gumroad. This means you must own the copyright or have the necessary permissions and licenses for any content you sell.
- Be aware of intellectual property laws, including copyright, trademark, and patent laws, to protect your own work and avoid infringing on others' rights.

Content Licensing

- Specify the terms and conditions of use for your digital products by creating a clear licensing agreement. This agreement outlines how customers can use the product, such as for personal use, commercial use, or redistribution.

- Consider using licenses such as Creative Commons licenses or custom licenses that meet your specific needs.

Terms of Service and Policies

- Draft comprehensive terms of service and policies for your Gumroad store. These should cover aspects like refunds, returns, privacy, and intellectual property rights.
- Make these policies easily accessible on your store and ensure customers agree to them before purchasing.

Privacy and Data Protection

- Comply with data protection regulations, such as GDPR (General Data Protection Regulation) and CCPA (California Consumer Privacy Act), when collecting and processing customer data.
- Clearly state your data handling practices and ensure customers' consent to your data collection and use.

Age Restrictions

- If your products have age restrictions, clearly communicate these limitations. For example, if you're selling adult content, you should require age verification before access.

- Implement mechanisms to restrict access to age-appropriate customers.

Tax Compliance

- Understand and comply with local and international tax laws related to digital product sales.
- Determine if you are required to collect and remit sales tax, VAT (Value Added Tax), or other taxes based on your location and the location of your customers.

Terms for Collaborations

- When collaborating with others, such as co-authors, artists, or developers, create clear agreements that outline revenue sharing, ownership, and intellectual property rights.
- Address potential disputes or issues that may arise from collaborations.

Disclaimer and Liability Limitation

- Include disclaimers in your product descriptions or terms of service to limit your liability, especially if your digital products provide advice or instructions.

- Clearly state that you are not providing legal, medical, or financial advice, and users should seek professional advice in those areas.

Digital Rights Management (DRM)

- Consider using DRM or watermarking to protect your digital products from unauthorized distribution or copying.
- Understand the limitations of DRM and how it may impact the user experience.

Legal Support and Documentation

- Consult with legal professionals, such as attorneys or intellectual property experts, to ensure your store's legal framework is sound.
- Maintain clear records of licenses, agreements, and correspondence related to your digital products.

Handling Copyright Infringements

- Have a process in place for addressing potential copyright infringements on Gumroad. This may include responding to takedown notices or resolving disputes with other creators or copyright holders.

Compliance with Gumroad's Policies

- Familiarize yourself with Gumroad's terms of service, community guidelines, and policies. Ensure your store and products align with Gumroad's guidelines to avoid potential account suspension or removal.

Keeping Up with Legal Changes

- Stay informed about changes in copyright laws, digital rights, and e-commerce regulations that may impact your Gumroad store.
- Be prepared to adapt your policies and practices to comply with evolving legal standards.

It's essential to take these legal and copyright considerations seriously to protect your intellectual property, maintain the trust of your customers, and operate your Gumroad store in compliance with the law. Consult with legal professionals for specific advice tailored to your business and product offerings.

SUCCESS STORIES AND CASE STUDIES

Success stories and case studies can provide valuable insights and inspiration for creators looking to thrive on Gumroad. Here are some success stories and case study subtopics to explore:

Notable Creators on Gumroad

- Profile successful creators who have built a substantial following and income on Gumroad.
- Learn from their strategies, product offerings, and marketing techniques.

Emerging Artists and Creators

- Highlight the journeys of new and lesser-known creators who have found success on Gumroad.
- Explore how they leveraged the platform to grow their audience and income.

Cross-Platform Success

- Examine creators who have successfully integrated Gumroad with other platforms like Patreon, YouTube, or social media.

- Understand how they diversified their income streams and expanded their reach.

Multi-Product Success

- Showcase creators who offer a variety of digital products, such as e-books, online courses, software, and more.
- Analyze how they managed and marketed their diverse product portfolio.

Niche Market Success

- Explore case studies of creators who have carved out a niche market for their digital products.
- Understand the advantages of catering to a specific audience.

Monetizing Free Content

- Learn from creators who have successfully monetized free content, such as free e-books or sample products, to drive sales of premium offerings.

Community Building and Engagement

- Investigate how creators have built engaged and supportive communities around their Gumroad stores.
- Explore the role of community in their success.

Effective Marketing Strategies

- Analyze the marketing strategies used by successful Gumroad creators, including content marketing, email campaigns, social media engagement, and influencer partnerships.

Scaling and Growth

- Study creators who have scaled their Gumroad businesses, whether by expanding their product catalog, hiring assistance, or exploring new niches.
- Understand how they managed growth while maintaining quality.

Leveraging Feedback

- Discover how creators have used customer feedback and reviews to improve their products and services.
- Understand the iterative process of product development.

Nonprofit and Cause-Related Success

- Explore success stories of creators who use Gumroad for fundraising and nonprofit initiatives.
- Understand how they combined their passion with digital products to make a positive impact.

Collaborative Success

- Examine creators who have found success through collaborations with other creators or businesses on Gumroad.
- Learn how they leveraged partnerships for mutual benefit.

Sustainability and Long-Term Success

- Study creators who have maintained a consistent and sustainable income over the long term through their Gumroad stores.
- Explore their strategies for sustaining their businesses.

Challenges and How They Overcame Them

- Understand the obstacles and setbacks that creators faced on Gumroad and how they overcame them.
- Gain insights into resilience and adaptability.

Adapting to Changing Trends

- Analyze how creators have adapted to changing trends in the digital creator economy, such as the rise of NFTs, web3, or new content formats.

- Explore their strategies for staying relevant.

These success stories and case studies can serve as valuable sources of inspiration and practical insights for creators looking to build their own success on Gumroad. By studying the journeys and strategies of others, you can adapt and implement the lessons learned to achieve your own goals on the platform.

PLATFORM UPDATES AND FEATURES

Staying up to date with platform updates and features on Gumroad is essential to make the most of the platform's capabilities and keep your digital products and store competitive. Here are some subtopics related to Gumroad platform updates and features:

Latest Feature Releases

Keep track of the most recent features and updates rolled out by Gumroad. This could include improvements to the user interface, new tools for creators, or enhancements to the customer experience.

Product Delivery and Management Updates

Explore updates that make it easier to manage and deliver digital products to your customers, such as streamlined file uploads or enhanced customization options.

Mobile App Enhancements

Stay informed about updates and improvements to Gumroad's mobile app, which allows you to manage your store and communicate with customers on the go.

Analytics and Reporting Features

Discover new analytics and reporting tools that help you track sales, customer behavior, and product performance. These insights can inform your decision-making.

Customer Communication Tools

Learn about communication features that help you engage with your customers more effectively, whether through updates, newsletters, or targeted messaging.

Subscription and Pre-order Improvements

Stay updated on changes that affect subscription products, pre-orders, or other monetization models offered on Gumroad.

Customization and Branding Updates

Explore features that allow you to customize your store and product pages to match your branding and style more precisely.

Security and Anti-Piracy Measures

Stay informed about security and anti-piracy features that help protect your digital products from unauthorized distribution.

Integration Options

Learn about new integrations and third-party tools that enhance your Gumroad experience, whether for marketing, analytics, or other aspects of your business.

Customer Experience Enhancements

Explore updates that improve the overall customer experience on Gumroad, such as changes to the checkout process or additional support options.

Internationalization and Multilingual Support

Stay informed about updates that enhance Gumroad's support for creators and customers from different regions and languages.

Payment Gateway Integration

Understand how Gumroad integrates with various payment gateways and whether new options are available.

Mobile and Web Accessibility

Stay updated on improvements to the mobile and web user experience for both creators and customers.

Educational Resources for Creators

Discover new educational materials and resources provided by Gumroad to help creators succeed on the platform, including webinars, guides, and tutorials.

Community and Support Updates

Explore changes to the Gumroad community, forums, and support options, as well as any updates to the platform's customer service.

User Feedback and Feature Requests

Keep an eye on user feedback and feature requests submitted by the Gumroad community. These may give you insights into upcoming changes and improvements.

API and Developer Updates

If you're a developer or want to build custom solutions, stay informed about updates to Gumroad's API and developer tools.

Beta Programs and Early Access

Consider participating in Gumroad's beta programs or early access features to test and provide feedback on new functionalities before they're widely released.

By actively following Gumroad's updates and features, you can leverage the platform's latest offerings to enhance your store, streamline your operations, and provide a better experience for your customers. Regularly visiting Gumroad's official website and community forums is a great way to stay informed about these developments.

COMMUNITY AND NETWORKING

Engaging with the Gumroad community and networking with other creators can be a valuable part of your journey on the platform. Here are some subtopics related to community and networking on Gumroad:

Gumroad Creator Community

- Join the official Gumroad creator community or forums to connect with fellow creators, share experiences, and exchange ideas.
- Participate in discussions and seek advice or feedback from the community.

Social Media Groups and Hashtags

- Find and join social media groups or use relevant hashtags where Gumroad creators gather.
- Use platforms like Twitter, Facebook, or Instagram to connect with a broader community.

Collaborative Projects

- Explore opportunities for collaborative projects with other Gumroad creators. Collaborations can help you reach new audiences and create unique products.
- Work on joint ventures, co-authored books, or co-developed courses with like-minded creators.

Cross-Promotion

- Establish partnerships with other creators for cross-promotion. Promote each other's products to your respective audiences.
- Cross-promotion can help boost sales and expand your reach.

Networking Events and Webinars

- Attend virtual networking events, webinars, or workshops organized by Gumroad or other creators.
- These events provide opportunities to learn from experts and connect with potential collaborators.

Mastermind Groups

- Form or join mastermind groups with other creators who have similar goals and interests.
- Regular group meetings can provide accountability and peer support.

Creator Showcases and Interviews

- Feature other creators on your blog, podcast, or social media to help showcase their work.
- Participate in interviews and showcases to increase your visibility within the Gumroad community.

Feedback and Critique

- Seek feedback and constructive critique from the Gumroad community on your products and store.
- Provide feedback to others to foster a supportive environment.

Engaging with Customers

- Interact with your customers on social media or through your Gumroad store.

- Create opportunities for engagement by responding to comments and messages.

Local or Niche Meetups

- Attend local or niche-specific meetups, conferences, or conventions relevant to your creative field.
- These in-person events can provide valuable networking opportunities.

Email Marketing Lists and Newsletters

- Build an email list of your loyal fans and customers. Communicate with your audience through newsletters and updates.
- Use email to foster a sense of community and provide exclusive content or offers.

Discord or Slack Communities

- Join or create Discord or Slack communities for Gumroad creators.
- Use these channels for real-time discussions, support, and collaboration.

Sharing Knowledge and Resources

- Share your knowledge and resources with the community, whether through blog posts, guides, or tutorials.
- Provide valuable insights to help other creators succeed.

Feedback Loops and Surveys

- Create feedback loops by conducting surveys or polls to collect input from your audience.
- Use the feedback to improve your products and store based on customer preferences.

Community Challenges and Contests

- Organize or participate in community challenges and contests to spark creativity and engagement.
- Encourage the creation and sharing of content within the community.

Building relationships and networking within the Gumroad community can help you stay motivated, find opportunities for growth, and collaborate with others to enhance your creative journey. It's a supportive environment where you can learn, share, and celebrate your successes together.

MONETIZATION STRATEGIES

Monetization strategies on Gumroad are essential for creators looking to generate income from their digital products. Here are various monetization strategies and subtopics to consider:

Selling Digital Products

- Offer your digital products for sale on Gumroad, such as e-books, artwork, music, software, templates, courses, and more.
- Determine the appropriate pricing model, whether it's fixed pricing, pay-what-you-want, or tiered pricing.

Membership and Subscription Models

- Create membership or subscription-based offerings that provide exclusive content, early access, or ongoing value to subscribers.
- Consider offering different subscription tiers with varying benefits.

Pre-orders and Crowdfunding

- Use Gumroad to set up pre-orders for upcoming products to generate interest and sales before the official release.

- Utilize crowdfunding campaigns to secure funding and engage with your community.

Bundling and Upselling

- Bundle related products together to increase the overall value of a purchase.
- Implement upsell strategies by offering additional products or premium versions during the checkout process.

Discounts and Limited-Time Offers

- Create urgency and boost sales with limited-time discounts, flash sales, or special offers.
- Offer discounts during holidays, special occasions, or to celebrate milestones.

Leveraging Free Content

- Use free content, such as free e-books, sample chapters, or free downloads, to attract a wider audience and drive sales of premium products.

Affiliate Programs

- Establish an affiliate program to incentivize others to promote your products in exchange for a commission.
- Collaborate with affiliates and provide them with marketing materials.

Digital Product Launches

- Plan well-executed product launches that include teaser campaigns, email marketing, social media promotions, and exclusive access for early buyers.

Fulfillment Models

- Choose between direct fulfillment, where customers receive the digital product immediately upon purchase, and delayed fulfillment, where customers get access at a specific time.

Diversifying Your Product Portfolio

- Offer a variety of digital products across different categories or niches.
- Experiment with various types of content to see what resonates with your audience.

Customer Loyalty Programs

- Reward loyal customers with perks like discounts, exclusive content, or early access.
- Encourage repeat purchases and referrals by offering incentives.

Custom Orders and Commission Work

- Accept custom orders or offer commission-based work if it aligns with your skills and creative field.
- Set clear terms and pricing for custom projects.

Sales and Revenue Reports

- Regularly review sales and revenue reports to gain insights into your most profitable products and customer behaviors.
- Use data to refine your monetization strategies.

Tiered Pricing and Upside Down Pricing

- Explore tiered pricing models where customers can choose different product versions or bundles based on their needs and budget.

- Consider upside-down pricing, where customers pay more as they find more value in your product.

Continuous Improvement

- Continuously refine your monetization strategies based on customer feedback, market trends, and changes in the digital creator landscape.
- Be adaptable and willing to try new approaches.

Niche Monetization

- Identify unique monetization opportunities within your niche or industry.
- Tailor your strategies to meet the specific needs and preferences of your target audience.

Tax Considerations and Pricing

- Account for taxes and fees in your pricing strategies, ensuring that you remain profitable after deductions.

Blockchain and NFT Monetization

- Stay informed about emerging monetization opportunities in the blockchain space, such as NFTs (Non-Fungible

Tokens), and explore how they can complement your existing strategy.

Effective monetization on Gumroad involves a combination of pricing strategies, marketing efforts, and ongoing adaptation to meet the evolving needs of your audience. Tailor your approach to your unique content and target audience to optimize your earnings on the platform.

TOOLS AND RESOURCES FOR CREATORS

There are various tools and resources available to creators that can help them succeed on platforms like Gumroad. These tools can assist with content creation, marketing, analytics, and more. Here are some subtopics related to tools and resources for creators on Gumroad:

Content Creation Tools

Explore software and tools for creating digital products, such as graphic design software, writing and editing tools, music production software, and coding platforms.

Digital Art and Design Resources

Access resources like stock photos, fonts, icons, and design templates to enhance the visual appeal of your products.

E-book and Document Creation Software

Utilize e-book and document creation software to publish and format digital books and documents professionally.

Audio and Video Editing Tools

Enhance the quality of your audio and video products with editing software and tools for sound and video production.

Email Marketing and List Building

Choose email marketing platforms and list-building tools to engage with your audience, send newsletters, and automate email campaigns.

Social Media Management

Use social media management tools to schedule posts, monitor engagement, and track your performance on various social platforms.

Keyword Research and SEO Tools

Optimize your Gumroad store and products for search engines with keyword research and SEO tools.

Analytics and Reporting Platforms

Track sales, customer behavior, and product performance with analytics and reporting tools.

Payment Processing and Financial Tools

Consider financial tools and platforms that facilitate payment processing, bookkeeping, and tax reporting.

Graphic Design Software

Invest in graphic design software for creating attractive product visuals and promotional materials.

Video Hosting and Streaming Services

Use video hosting and streaming platforms to deliver video content to your audience securely.

Web Hosting and Website Builders

Build a professional website and host it with web hosting services or website builders to showcase your products and brand.

Project Management and Collaboration Tools

Collaborate effectively with teams or partners using project management and collaboration platforms.

Affiliate Marketing and Partnership Tools

Manage your affiliate marketing programs or partnership collaborations using affiliate tracking and management tools.

Podcast Hosting Platforms

Host and distribute your podcasts with dedicated podcast hosting platforms.

Content Marketing Resources

Access content marketing resources, such as content calendars, marketing templates, and content creation guides.

Educational and Course Creation Platforms

Explore e-learning and course creation platforms to design and sell online courses.

Legal and Copyright Resources

Utilize legal and copyright resources, including templates for terms of service, privacy policies, and licensing agreements.

Blockchain and NFT Tools

Stay informed about tools and resources related to blockchain, NFT creation, and digital asset management.

Community and Networking Groups

Join online communities and forums for creators to network, share insights, and seek advice.

Educational Content and Tutorials

Access educational content and tutorials that can help you improve your skills and navigate the digital creator landscape.

Podcasts and Books for Creators

Listen to podcasts or read books that provide valuable insights and strategies for creators.

Funding and Crowdfunding Platforms

Explore crowdfunding and fundraising platforms to secure funds for your creative projects.

Webinars and Online Workshops

Participate in webinars and online workshops to gain new knowledge and skills.

Financial and Tax Advisory Services

Consider seeking the services of financial and tax advisors to manage your income, taxes, and financial planning.

Blockchain and NFT Education

Explore educational resources and courses that teach you about blockchain technology, NFTs, and how they can be integrated into your creative work.

Select the tools and resources that align with your creative goals, content type, and target audience. Continuously evaluate and update your toolkit to adapt to changing trends and remain competitive on platforms like Gumroad.

CONTENT CREATION AND PRODUCT DEVELOPMENT

Creating compelling content and developing digital products are at the core of a successful Gumroad store. Here are subtopics related to content creation and product development:

Choosing Your Niche and Audience

Define your target audience and niche. Understand their needs, preferences, and pain points.

Idea Generation and Research

- Research market trends, customer demands, and competitors to generate product ideas.
- Validate your ideas by assessing their potential demand.

Content Planning and Outlining

- Create a detailed plan or outline for your digital product, whether it's an e-book, course, or software.
- Organize your content into a logical structure.

Content Creation Tools

Choose the appropriate tools and software for content creation, whether it's graphic design, writing, audio, video, or code.

Writing and Editing

Write high-quality content for e-books, articles, or scripts, and invest in professional editing or proofreading when necessary.

Design and Multimedia Production

- Design visually appealing graphics, images, and multimedia elements for your digital products.
- Use software like Adobe Creative Cloud for graphic design or Adobe Premiere Pro for video editing.

Audio and Video Production

- Create audio products, such as podcasts or music tracks, and produce high-quality video content for courses or tutorials.
- Invest in recording and editing equipment or software.

Course Curriculum and Lesson Planning

- Develop a well-structured curriculum for online courses with clear learning objectives.
- Plan lessons, assignments, and assessments effectively.

Software Development and Coding

Code and develop software, plugins, or applications, and ensure they are well-documented and user-friendly.

Digital Art and Visual Content

Produce digital art and illustrations for sale as downloadable products or physical prints.

Quality Assurance and Testing

Thoroughly test your software, courses, or digital products to ensure they are error-free and provide a seamless user experience.

Feedback and Iteration

- Collect feedback from peers or beta testers and make improvements based on their suggestions.
- Continuously iterate on your products to enhance their quality.

Content Monetization Strategies

Decide on the monetization strategy for your content, whether it's through direct sales, subscriptions, crowdfunding, or a combination of methods.

Digital Asset Management

Organize your digital assets, including images, videos, documents, and code, for easy access and future use.

Packaging and Bundling

Consider packaging multiple related products together as bundles to increase their perceived value.

Metadata and Descriptions

Write compelling and informative metadata, descriptions, and titles for your products to enhance discoverability and conversion rates.

Testing User Experience

Test the user experience of accessing and using your digital products to ensure they are user-friendly and intuitive.

Legal Considerations

Ensure that you have the necessary rights and permissions for all content used in your products, and establish clear licensing terms.

Content Promotion

Develop a content promotion strategy that includes pre-launch, launch, and post-launch marketing efforts.

Interactive and Engaging Content

Explore methods to make your content interactive and engaging, such as quizzes, assessments, or gamified elements.

Accessibility and Inclusivity

Consider accessibility features for your content, ensuring that it's usable by people with disabilities.

Creating Content for Multiple Platforms

- Adapt your content for various platforms, such as social media, blogs, or different e-book formats, to reach a wider audience.

Successful content creation and product development require careful planning, dedication, and a deep understanding of your target audience. Continuously improving your skills, seeking feedback, and staying updated on industry trends are essential for success on Gumroad.

DESIGN AND BRANDING

Design and branding are crucial aspects of creating a memorable and appealing Gumroad store that attracts customers. Here are subtopics related to design and branding:

Logo and Visual Identity

- Create a unique and recognizable logo for your brand.
- Establish a visual identity that includes consistent colors, fonts, and design elements.

Store and Product Page Design

- Design your Gumroad store and product pages to be visually appealing and user-friendly.
- Use high-quality images and graphics to showcase your products.

Branding Guidelines

- Develop branding guidelines that outline how your brand should be represented, ensuring consistency in all your marketing materials.

Customer-Centric Design

- Prioritize user experience and customer-centric design to make it easy for customers to navigate your store and make purchases.

Mobile and Responsive Design

- Ensure that your Gumroad store and product pages are optimized for mobile devices to reach a broader audience.

Customizing Your Store

- Customize the appearance of your Gumroad store to reflect your brand's personality and style.

Aesthetics and Visual Appeal

- Pay attention to aesthetics and visual appeal in all aspects of your store, from product images to the layout of your storefront.

Typography and Fonts

- Choose fonts that align with your brand's personality and are easy to read.

- Maintain consistency in font usage across your store and materials.

Color Schemes

- Select a color scheme that resonates with your brand's identity and values.
- Use colors strategically to create visual impact and evoke emotions.

Images and Graphics

- Use high-quality images and graphics that relate to your products and reinforce your brand's message.

Product Packaging and Presentation

- Create visually appealing packaging for your digital products, including cover images for e-books, course thumbnails, and promotional graphics.

Product Mockups

- Use product mockups to showcase how your digital products will be used or experienced.

- This is particularly useful for visualizing e-books, software, or templates.

Branded Merchandise

- Consider offering branded merchandise like T-shirts, stickers, or posters to promote your brand and products.

Consistency Across Platforms

- Ensure that your branding is consistent across all your online platforms, including social media, your website, and Gumroad.

Storytelling and Brand Narrative

- Craft a compelling brand story and narrative that engages customers and conveys the essence of your brand.

Customer Engagement

- Encourage customer engagement by using appealing visuals and graphics in your social media posts and email campaigns.

Feedback and Testing

- Seek feedback on your design and branding elements from peers, customers, or design professionals.
- A/B test different design elements to optimize your store's conversion rate.

Accessibility and Inclusivity

- Ensure that your design and branding are inclusive and accessible to a wide range of users, including those with disabilities.

Updating and Evolving

- Regularly review and update your design and branding to stay relevant and adapt to changing trends or customer preferences.

Competitive Analysis

- Analyze the branding and design choices of successful competitors or creators in your niche to gain insights and inspiration.

Effective design and branding not only make your Gumroad store visually appealing but also help establish a strong and memorable brand identity. When customers encounter a consistent and aesthetically pleasing brand, they are more likely to trust your products and continue to engage with your content.

CUSTOMER ENGAGEMENT AND COMMUNITY BUILDING

Building customer engagement and a strong community around your Gumroad store is essential for long-term success. Here are subtopics related to customer engagement and community building:

Customer Communication

- Maintain open and consistent communication with your customers through email newsletters, updates, and social media.
- Respond promptly to customer inquiries and feedback.

Engaging Content Creation

- Create content that resonates with your audience and encourages interaction, whether through blog posts, videos, or social media posts.

Community Forums and Groups

- Establish community forums or social media groups where customers and fans can connect, share their experiences, and discuss your products.

- Actively participate in these communities to foster engagement.

Engagement on Social Media

- Use social media platforms to engage with your audience, share behind-the-scenes content, and initiate conversations with followers.

Webinars and Live Events

- Host webinars, live Q&A sessions, or live product demonstrations to engage with your audience in real-time.
- Encourage audience participation and questions during these events.

Feedback and Surveys

- Collect feedback and insights from your customers through surveys, polls, and questionnaires.
- Use this feedback to improve your products and services.

Loyalty Programs

- Create loyalty programs or offer incentives for repeat customers, such as exclusive content, discounts, or early access to new products.

User-Generated Content

- Encourage customers to share their experiences with your products through reviews, testimonials, and user-generated content.
- Feature this content on your Gumroad store.

Email Marketing

- Utilize email marketing to send targeted content, promotions, and updates to your subscribers.
- Segment your email list to provide personalized content to different customer groups.

Exclusive Content for Subscribers

- Offer exclusive content or perks to subscribers to incentivize them to join your mailing list or subscribe to your products.

Customer Surveys and Research

- Conduct research to understand your audience's preferences, needs, and pain points.
- Use this information to tailor your products and content.

Crowdsourcing and Co-Creation

- Involve your community in product development decisions or creative projects.
- Crowdsourcing ideas and involving them in co-creation can increase customer engagement.

Virtual Events and Workshops

- Host virtual events, workshops, or training sessions related to your niche.
- These events can serve as a platform for knowledge-sharing and community building.

Engagement Metrics and Analytics

- Analyze engagement metrics such as social media interactions, email open rates, and customer participation in events.
- Use these insights to refine your engagement strategies.

Customer Support and Service

- Offer exceptional customer support, addressing inquiries and issues promptly.
- Make customers feel valued and appreciated.

Inclusivity and Diversity

- Promote an inclusive and diverse community that welcomes individuals of all backgrounds and identities.

Conflict Resolution

- Establish guidelines for conflict resolution within your community and ensure a respectful and safe environment for all participants.

Consistency and Persistence

- Consistently engage with your audience and persist in your efforts to build a strong community.
- Over time, your community will grow and become more engaged.

Networking and Collaborations

- Collaborate with other creators or businesses to expand your network and introduce your community to new experiences and products.

Measuring Community Growth

- Track the growth and activity of your community over time.
- Set measurable goals for community engagement and evaluate your progress.

Effective customer engagement and community building can foster loyalty, increase sales, and turn one-time customers into dedicated fans. Creating a supportive and engaged community can help your Gumroad store thrive over the long term.

TECHNICAL INTEGRATION AND AUTOMATION

Technical integration and automation can streamline your Gumroad store's operations, making it more efficient and helping you manage various aspects of your business. Here are subtopics related to technical integration and automation:

Payment Processing Integration

- Integrate your Gumroad store with payment gateways to facilitate smooth and secure transactions.
- Choose from various payment processors, including PayPal, Stripe, and more.

Email Marketing Integration

- Connect your Gumroad account with email marketing platforms like MailChimp, ConvertKit, or MailerLite to automate email campaigns, subscriber lists, and customer communications.

Analytics and Reporting Tools:

- Integrate analytics and reporting tools to track the performance of your store, including sales data, customer behavior, and product insights.

Content Delivery Automation

- Automate the delivery of digital products to customers upon purchase, ensuring a seamless and instant experience.
- Implement autoresponders to send follow-up emails with product download links.

Inventory Management

- Set up inventory management systems to track product availability, restock items automatically, and avoid overselling.

Customer Relationship Management (CRM) Integration

- Connect your Gumroad store to a CRM system to manage customer relationships, track interactions, and segment your customer base for targeted marketing.

Affiliate Marketing Platforms

- Use affiliate marketing platforms to automate your affiliate program, track referrals, and manage affiliate payouts.

Marketing Automation

- Implement marketing automation tools to schedule and automate social media posts, email campaigns, and promotional activities.
- Set up autoresponders for triggered marketing campaigns based on customer actions.

eCommerce Platform Integration

- If you have an existing eCommerce website, integrate Gumroad for additional product offerings or for selling digital products alongside physical items.

Zapier and Third-Party Integrations

- Use platforms like Zapier to connect Gumroad with a wide range of other apps and services for more advanced automation.

- Automate workflows between Gumroad and tools like Google Sheets, Slack, and Trello.

Order Fulfillment and Shipping Integration

- Integrate your Gumroad store with order fulfillment and shipping systems if you sell physical products or merchandise.
- Automate the shipping process and tracking updates.

Subscription and Membership Management

- Use subscription and membership management platforms to automate recurring billing, member access, and content delivery for subscribers.

Bookkeeping and Financial Automation

- Implement accounting software or services to automate financial tasks, track revenue, and generate financial reports.
- Simplify tax preparation with automated income tracking.

Security and Anti-Piracy Measures

- Automate the implementation of security measures to protect your digital products from unauthorized distribution and piracy.
- Use digital rights management (DRM) solutions if necessary.

Website and Landing Page Integration

- Integrate Gumroad with your website or landing pages to seamlessly embed product listings, checkout options, and payment processing.

Custom API Development

- Develop custom API solutions to automate specific tasks or connect Gumroad with unique systems.
- Consider hiring developers to create bespoke integrations.

Compliance and Legal Automation

- Automate legal compliance tasks, such as generating terms of service and privacy policies, to ensure your store operates within the law.

Backup and Data Recovery

- Set up automated backup and data recovery solutions to protect your store's data in case of system failures or data loss.

Regular Software Updates

- Ensure that your software and integrations are regularly updated to benefit from the latest features and security patches.

Effective technical integration and automation can save you time, reduce manual effort, and improve the overall customer experience. It allows you to focus on creating content and growing your Gumroad store while streamlining operations and ensuring a professional and efficient online presence.

LOCALIZED SELLING AND MULTILINGUAL SUPPORT

Localized selling and providing multilingual support on Gumroad can expand your reach to a global audience and enhance the customer experience for non-English-speaking customers. Here are subtopics related to localized selling and multilingual support:

Localization Strategy

- Develop a localization strategy that outlines the regions and languages you want to target with your products.

Multi-Currency Pricing

- Offer multi-currency pricing options to make it easier for international customers to understand product costs and complete transactions in their preferred currency.

Language Options

- Provide product descriptions, titles, and customer communication in multiple languages to accommodate non-English-speaking customers.

International Payment Methods

- Accept a variety of international payment methods to ensure customers can make purchases using their preferred payment options.

Localized Product Descriptions

- Translate and adapt product descriptions to cater to the cultural nuances and preferences of specific regions or markets.

Custom Landing Pages

- Create custom landing pages or product pages for different language groups or regions.
- Optimize them for search engines in each target language.

Geographic Targeting:

- Use geographic targeting to display different content or products to users based on their location.
- This can help you tailor your offerings to local interests and needs.

Customer Support in Multiple Languages

- Offer customer support in multiple languages to assist customers with inquiries and issues.

- Ensure your support team can communicate effectively in the languages you target.

Localized Marketing Campaigns

- Develop marketing campaigns that are culturally relevant to specific regions and languages.

- Tailor your content and imagery to resonate with local audiences.

SEO and Localization

- Optimize your Gumroad store and product pages for local search engines by researching keywords and ensuring that your content ranks well in local search results.

Local Social Media Presence

- Build a presence on local or region-specific social media platforms to reach potential customers more effectively.

Translation and Localization Tools

- Use translation and localization tools, software, or services to streamline the translation process and ensure accuracy.
- Consider hiring professional translators for high-quality results.

Legal and Tax Considerations

- Comply with local tax regulations and legal requirements when selling internationally.
- Understand VAT, GST, or other regional tax obligations.

Cultural Sensitivity

- Be sensitive to cultural differences, customs, and local preferences in your marketing materials and communication.

Localized Pricing and Discounts

- Offer region-specific pricing and discounts to match the economic conditions of different markets.

Testing and Localization Feedback

- Test your localized content and features with native speakers or local experts to ensure cultural and linguistic accuracy.

Localization of Customer Education

- Provide educational resources, such as tutorials or FAQs, in multiple languages to help customers understand your products and how to use them.

Continuous Monitoring and Adaptation

- Regularly monitor the performance of your localized efforts and be prepared to adapt to changing market dynamics and customer needs.

By effectively implementing localized selling and multilingual support, you can broaden your customer base and create a more inclusive and accessible experience for individuals around the world. This approach allows you to tap into new markets and connect with customers who prefer to interact in their native language.

GUMROAD ALTERNATIVES AND COMPARISONS

Gumroad is a popular platform for selling digital products, but there are several alternatives available, each with its own features and pricing. Here are some Gumroad alternatives and comparisons:

Shopify

- Shopify is a comprehensive e-commerce platform that allows you to sell physical and digital products.
- While Shopify is more versatile, Gumroad is specifically tailored for digital creators and offers a simpler setup for digital products.

Etsy

- Etsy is a marketplace for handmade and vintage goods. It's a great choice for selling digital artwork, printables, and craft-related digital products.
- Gumroad provides more control over your store and branding.

SendOwl

- SendOwl is another platform for selling digital products, with features like secure delivery and subscriptions.
- Gumroad is known for its ease of use and might be more user-friendly for some creators.

Selz

- Selz is an e-commerce platform that supports both digital and physical products. It includes features for building an online store.
- Gumroad is focused on simplicity and digital products, making it more streamlined for digital creators.

PayHip

- PayHip is a platform for selling digital downloads, memberships, and subscriptions.
- It's comparable to Gumroad in terms of digital product sales, but Gumroad has a broader user base.

Podia

- Podia is a platform for selling digital products and online courses. It includes features for hosting and delivering online courses.
- Gumroad is more lightweight and straightforward, while Podia is suitable for more complex offerings.

Teachable

- Teachable is primarily for creating and selling online courses. It offers in-depth course-building features.
- Gumroad is simpler and better suited for creators who don't need a full-fledged course platform.

Sellfy

- Sellfy is another platform for selling digital products and subscriptions, with built-in marketing and customization features.
- Gumroad has a stronger focus on simplicity and user-friendliness.

FastSpring

- FastSpring is an e-commerce platform specializing in software and SaaS sales. It's more oriented towards businesses and software companies.
- Gumroad is more accessible for individual creators and artists.

Big Cartel

- Big Cartel is a platform designed for artists and makers to sell art and handmade products.
- Gumroad is more flexible for digital creators and offers a broader range of product types.

WooCommerce (with WordPress)

- WooCommerce is a plugin for WordPress that turns your website into an e-commerce store.
- While versatile, it requires more technical expertise to set up and maintain compared to Gumroad.

When choosing a platform, consider your specific needs, such as the types of products you're selling, your technical skills, and your budget. Some creators prefer Gumroad for its simplicity and focus on digital products, while others opt for more comprehensive e-commerce solutions like Shopify for their broader range of offerings.

GUMROAD FOR NONPROFITS AND FUNDRAISING

Gumroad can be a valuable platform for nonprofits and fundraising efforts, enabling organizations to sell digital products, raise funds, and support their missions. Here are subtopics related to using Gumroad for nonprofits and fundraising:

Product Creation and Sale

- Nonprofits can create and sell digital products, such as e-books, guides, templates, or artwork, to generate funds.
- These products can be designed to align with the nonprofit's mission or to provide value to donors.

Donation Pages

- Gumroad allows you to create donation pages where supporters can contribute directly to your cause.
- Customize donation pages with branding, imagery, and clear messaging about your nonprofit's goals.

Recurring Donations

- Set up recurring donation options, enabling supporters to make regular contributions to your organization.
- This can provide a steady stream of income for your nonprofit.

Membership and Subscription Models

- Create membership or subscription programs that offer exclusive content, benefits, or early access to donors who support your nonprofit on an ongoing basis.

Crowdfunding Campaigns

- Use Gumroad to set up crowdfunding campaigns to raise a specific amount of funds for a project, event, or initiative.
- Communicate campaign progress and offer rewards to contributors.

Digital Art and Creative Fundraising

- Encourage artists and creators to contribute digital art, music, or other creative works for fundraising purposes.

- Sell these works on Gumroad, with proceeds going to your nonprofit.

Transparency and Accountability

- Be transparent about how funds are used and the impact they have on your organization's mission.
- Share progress reports and stories that demonstrate the positive results of donations.

Affiliate Marketing

- Establish an affiliate program that allows supporters and influencers to promote your digital products or donation campaigns in exchange for a commission.

Email Marketing and Engagement

- Use email marketing to engage with your supporters, keep them informed about your nonprofit's activities, and encourage donations.

Localized Fundraising

- Appeal to international donors by offering multi-currency options and localized fundraising campaigns.

- Translate content to accommodate non-English-speaking supporters.

Digital Resource Libraries

- Create digital libraries of resources related to your nonprofit's cause, which can be offered to donors as a valuable incentive for contributions.

Virtual Events and Workshops

- Host virtual events, webinars, and workshops related to your cause, charging participation fees and using Gumroad for ticket sales.

Legal and Tax Compliance

- Ensure that your nonprofit complies with legal and tax regulations regarding fundraising and donations.

Public Relations and Outreach

- Use Gumroad to sell tickets or access to special events, with proceeds going toward your nonprofit.
- Collaborate with influencers and other organizations to expand your reach.

Data Security and Privacy

- Safeguard donor data and privacy to build trust with your supporters.
- Implement secure payment processing methods and data handling practices.

Accessibility and Inclusivity

- Ensure that your fundraising efforts are accessible to individuals with disabilities, and provide options for diverse payment methods and languages.

Gumroad can serve as a versatile tool for nonprofits to raise funds, engage with supporters, and advance their mission. Whether you're selling digital products, collecting donations, or hosting events, Gumroad can help you connect with a global audience and make a positive impact on your cause.

DIGITAL PRODUCT SECURITY AND ANTI-PIRACY MEASURES

Ensuring the security of your digital products and implementing effective anti-piracy measures is crucial to protect your intellectual property and revenue on platforms like Gumroad. Here are subtopics related to digital product security and anti-piracy measures:

Secure File Hosting

- Host your digital products on secure servers or cloud storage with access controls and encryption to prevent unauthorized downloads.

Watermarking

- Watermark images or documents with your logo or copyright information to deter piracy and protect your content.

File Encryption

- Encrypt digital products to make it difficult for unauthorized users to access or share your files without the appropriate decryption key.

Limited Downloads

- Restrict the number of times a customer can download a digital product to reduce the chances of unauthorized sharing.

Password Protection

- Use password protection for digital product files, allowing access only to customers who have the correct password.

Unique Download Links

- Generate unique download links for each customer to prevent link sharing and unauthorized access.

DRM (Digital Rights Management)

- Consider using DRM solutions to protect your digital products, although it can be complex and may impact the user experience.

Expiry Dates

- Set expiration dates for download links or access to digital products to limit their availability.

License Keys

- Provide license keys or serial numbers for software or digital products, which can help track and control usage.

Customer Data Collection

- Collect customer data during the purchase process, such as email addresses, to monitor and address misuse.

Legal Measures

- Include clear terms of service, copyright notices, and licensing agreements to establish your rights and clarify how your products can be used.

DMCA Takedown Notices

- Be prepared to issue Digital Millennium Copyright Act (DMCA) takedown notices to platforms hosting pirated copies of your products.

Monitoring and Reporting

- Use monitoring tools to track the distribution of your digital products on unauthorized websites or platforms.

- Report instances of piracy to relevant authorities or take legal action when necessary.

Community Engagement

- Build a supportive community and encourage your customers to report instances of piracy.
- Engage with your audience to educate them about the impact of piracy.

Product Updates

- Offer regular product updates or revisions to incentivize legitimate purchases rather than seeking pirated versions.

Customer Support and Education

- Provide excellent customer support to encourage customers to purchase genuine copies and educate them on the consequences of piracy.

Public Awareness

- Raise public awareness about the negative impacts of piracy on content creators and the importance of supporting artists and creators.

Blockchain and NFTs

- Explore blockchain technology and NFTs (Non-Fungible Tokens) to secure ownership of digital assets and limit unauthorized distribution.

Legal Action

- Consider taking legal action against individuals or platforms engaged in piracy if necessary and when feasible.

It's important to strike a balance between protecting your digital products and providing a seamless user experience for your legitimate customers. Implementing a combination of these security and anti-piracy measures can help safeguard your content and revenue on Gumroad and other platforms.

MOBILE AND APP INTEGRATION

Mobile and app integration can enhance your Gumroad store's accessibility and reach, making it more convenient for customers to access your digital products. Here are subtopics related to mobile and app integration:

Mobile Optimization

- Ensure that your Gumroad store is mobile-responsive, offering a user-friendly experience on smartphones and tablets.

Mobile Apps

- Develop or utilize mobile apps for your Gumroad store to provide a dedicated and convenient mobile shopping experience.

iOS and Android Apps

- Create both iOS and Android apps to cover a broad range of mobile users.

Push Notifications

- Implement push notification features in your app to alert users about new product releases, discounts, or promotions.

In-App Purchases

- Enable in-app purchases for your digital products, allowing customers to buy directly from your mobile app.

Authentication and User Accounts

- Implement secure authentication and user account management in your app, enabling customers to access their purchased products and account information.

Mobile Payment Options

Ensure that your app supports mobile payment methods, such as Apple Pay and Google Pay, to simplify the checkout process.

Offline Access

- Enable offline access to purchased digital products, allowing customers to access their content without an internet connection.

Multi-Platform Integration

- Integrate your mobile app with other platforms and marketplaces where your digital products are available for sale.

Cross-Device Sync

- Allow customers to sync their purchases and progress across multiple devices, providing a seamless experience.

API Integration

- Use Gumroad's API to integrate your mobile app with your Gumroad store, enabling real-time product updates and synchronization.

Content Streaming

- If your digital products are videos or music, implement streaming capabilities in your app to enhance the viewing and listening experience.

Offline Caching

- Use offline caching to store product information on users' devices, reducing load times and improving performance.

Geolocation and Location-Based Features

- Incorporate geolocation features to provide location-specific content, promotions, or event notifications.

App Store Optimization (ASO)

- Optimize your app's listing in app stores with keywords, descriptions, and visuals to enhance its discoverability.

User Ratings and Reviews

- Encourage satisfied customers to leave positive ratings and reviews in app stores to boost your app's credibility.

App Updates

- Regularly update your mobile app to fix bugs, improve performance, and introduce new features or enhancements.

User Support

- Offer responsive customer support within the app to address inquiries or issues quickly.

Accessibility Features

- Ensure your app is accessible to users with disabilities, adhering to accessibility guidelines and standards.

App Marketing

- Develop a marketing strategy to promote your mobile app to existing and potential customers.

Integrating mobile and app solutions with your Gumroad store can provide a seamless and convenient experience for your customers, increasing the likelihood of sales and customer satisfaction. Consider the preferences of your target audience and the types of digital products you sell when implementing mobile and app integration strategies.

EVOLVING TRENDS IN THE DIGITAL CREATOR ECONOMY

The digital creator economy is a dynamic and ever-evolving space, influenced by changing technologies, consumer behaviors, and market trends. Here are some of the evolving trends in the digital creator economy:

NFTs and Digital Collectibles

- Non-Fungible Tokens (NFTs) have gained significant attention, allowing creators to tokenize and sell digital art, collectibles, and other unique digital assets.

Web3 and Blockchain Technology

- The concept of Web3 is emerging, driven by decentralized technologies like blockchain, offering creators new opportunities for ownership, control, and monetization of their content.

Livestreaming and Virtual Events

- Creators are increasingly turning to livestreaming platforms to engage with their audience, host virtual events, and monetize live content.

Community Building

- The focus on building communities around creators and their content has grown, enabling closer connections between creators and their audiences.

Subscription Models

- Creators are adopting subscription-based monetization models, offering exclusive content, perks, and early access to subscribers.

Microtransactions and Tipping

- Microtransactions and tipping features are becoming more common, allowing fans to directly support creators with small contributions.

Content Monetization Platforms

- Platforms like Patreon, Ko-fi, and OnlyFans continue to evolve, offering creators various monetization options beyond traditional advertising and product sales.

AI-Generated Content

- AI is being used to assist creators in content generation, from generating music and art to automating certain aspects of content creation.

AR and VR Integration

- Augmented Reality (AR) and Virtual Reality (VR) are becoming tools for immersive storytelling and content experiences.

Inclusivity and Diversity

- The push for inclusivity and diversity in the creator space is driving more opportunities for underrepresented voices and perspectives.

Educational Content

- Creators are increasingly offering online courses, tutorials, and educational content, catering to a growing demand for self-improvement and skill development.

Short-Form Video

- Short-form video platforms like TikTok and Instagram Reels have gained prominence, providing creators with new ways to reach and engage with audiences.

Remote Collaboration

- Collaboration between creators and businesses is growing, with more brands seeking partnerships with digital creators for marketing and content creation.

Sustainability and Eco-Friendly Practices

- Creators are adopting eco-friendly practices and advocating for sustainability in content creation and product development.

Mental Health and Wellbeing

- There's a growing awareness of the mental health challenges that come with being a digital creator, and more emphasis is being placed on self-care and balance.

Regulatory Changes

- Creators are navigating changing regulations around online content, including copyright, data privacy, and advertising practices.

Livelihood Diversification

- Creators are diversifying their income sources, whether through multiple platforms, merchandise sales, or consulting services.

The Metaverse

- The concept of the metaverse, a virtual collective space where users interact, create content, and engage, is gaining attention, potentially opening new avenues for creators.

Emerging Content Niches

- New content niches are constantly emerging, driven by evolving trends and audience interests.

AI Content Moderation

- AI-powered content moderation is becoming more sophisticated, helping creators and platforms manage content and user interactions.

Adapting to these trends and staying updated on the evolving landscape of the digital creator economy is essential for success in this dynamic and competitive space. Creators who embrace innovation, engage with their audience, and stay agile in response to changing trends are likely to thrive in this creative and entrepreneurial environment.

CONCLUSION

Gumroad is a versatile and user-friendly platform that empowers digital creators and entrepreneurs to sell and market their digital products. Whether you're an artist, writer, musician, or any other type of creator, Gumroad provides the tools and features needed to reach a global audience and monetize your work effectively.

Gumroad's ease of use, customizable storefronts, and payment processing capabilities make it a popular choice for individuals and small businesses looking to sell digital products, memberships, or even fundraise for charitable causes. The platform's flexibility allows creators to implement a wide range of monetization strategies and integrate various tools to enhance their business operations.

With a commitment to providing creators with the means to build engaged communities, protect their digital assets, and adapt to emerging trends, Gumroad remains a valuable resource in the ever-evolving digital creator economy. By leveraging Gumroad's features and staying attuned to the latest industry trends, creators can find success and fulfillment in sharing their work with the world.

www.ingramcontent.com/pod-product-compliance
Lightning Source LLC
Chambersburg PA
CBHW062320290526
45794CB00005B/1841